Copyright 2020 - by Beth Costanzo

Whether you are visiting a zoo or taking a hike in the woods, there are countless numbers of animals that you can spot. If you're lucky enough, you may even be able to get a picture that you can share with friends and family.

ENTER THE FOREST IF YOU DARE!

www.adventuresofscubajack.com

Having said that, there are other types of animals that are legendary. Some people have claimed to have spotted them, but these specific animals are mostly considered to be myths. If you saw them in the wild, you would certainly want to document it. You could even become famous by seeing these animals and taking pictures of them.

In this article, we want to talk about one of those legendary animals. That animal is ***Bigfoot***.

Bigfoot is a legendary creature that lives in the wilderness. There is a vast amount of forest that has not been explored, and it is thought that Bigfoot resides there. When you are wandering through the forest, there is a chance that you may spot this legendary creature.

Even if you aren't able to spot Bigfoot in the wild, it is interesting to learn about Bigfoot's history and physical qualities. With this knowledge in hand, you can be prepared to not only spot Bigfoot, but to share some fascinating facts about Bigfoot to your family members and friends.

SOME BASIC FACTS ABOUT BIGFOOT

Bigfoot (who is also known as Sasquatch) is a legendary creature that is quite scary and intimidating. Those who have apparently seen him claim that he is around six to nine feet. He stands on two legs and is covered in hair. His hair color has been described as black, dark brown, or dark red. He is also known to give off a foul smell and can move silently through the woods. Finally, Bigfoot's weight is in question, but it is estimated that he weighs about 400 to 1,000 pounds.

One of the most notable attributes of Bigfoot is its *large feet and footprints*. These footprints are as large as 24 inches long and eight inches wide. These are really large footprints and should catch your eye if you are hiking or walking in the woods. If you see them in the forest, however, they may be hard to distinguish with other big animals like bears. Nevertheless, be careful, as Bigfoot or a bear may be right around the corner!

Along with its footprints, Bigfoot allegedly is a fan of *vocalizations*. This means that Bigfoot has been heard grunting, whistling, and screaming. This means that you'll want to keep your ears open when you are hiking in the forest. A distant grunt or whistle may not be a familiar animal.

Instead, it may be Bigfoot making his presence known. Bigfoot has also been known to eat clams or shake trees. He is also thought to create unusual tree structures to mark his territory.

From his physical characteristics and behavior, let's talk about the *legend of Bigfoot*. Some cultures have shared stories about "wild men" or "hairy men" that walk through forests. In the year 1898, in fact, a chief of the Nlaka'pamux tribe told a story about a "wild man" shaking trees and eating clams. Members of different tribes told similar stories. Many of these early stories were collected and shared in a series of Canadian newspaper articles.

The first documented sighting of Bigfoot, however, allegedly occurred in 1967. Roger Patterson and Robert Gimlin recorded a short video that allegedly shows Bigfoot. The video was filmed in Northern California. Specifically, it occurred alongside Bluff Creek in Del Norte County, which is 38 miles south of Oregon and 18 miles east of the Pacific Ocean. The film itself runs for about one minute and seemingly shows a large, hairy, and bipedal creature glancing over its shoulder and disappearing and reappearing into trees. Even though plenty of people have tried to authenticate or debunk the film footage, it is still unclear whether the large hairy creature was actually Bigfoot.

The Patterson-Gimlin film is the most famous recording that is thought to be of Bigfoot. There have been other alleged sightings of the creature, but it is still unclear whether it *was actually* Bigfoot. Many of these potential sightings are located in the Pacific Northwest. This includes states like Washington, Oregon, and California. However, there have been other alleged sightings of Bigfoot across the United States.

Whenever we're talking about Bigfoot, it is always worth mentioning that many scientists are skeptical. They believe that these potential sightings of Bigfoot are either hoaxes or are misidentified animals (like bears). At this time, we cannot be sure whether Bigfoot is walking the forests of the United States. Those that believe Bigfoot isn't real also claim that Bigfoot is the counterpart to the Abominable Snowman. The Abominable Snowman, also known as the *Yeti*, is a mythical monster that is found in the Himalayan mountains in Asia.

However, that hasn't stopped people from believing in the legend of Bigfoot. One survey of Americans showed that more people believe in Bigfoot than they do in the *Big Bang Theory*.

Jane Goodall, who is a very famous primatologist, once said that she believes that they may exist. Along with this, several organizations are dedicated to researching and investigating Bigfoot. One of those organizations is the Bigfoot Field Researchers Organization. This organization includes reports from all around the United States about potential Bigfoot sightings.

The Legend Lives On

In the end, the *Legend of Bigfoot* persists. People across the United States and Canada have been sharing stories about Bigfoot for decades. Some argue that they have recorded real evidence of Bigfoot on film. Others simply tell stories where they saw a large, hairy creature walking on two legs around the woods.

We cannot be certain. However, if you are hiking in some wooded areas (particularly in the Pacific Northwest), there is a chance that you might spot him. Because of this, you definitely want to keep your eyes peeled. ***You never know if he is going to cross your path!***

BIGFOOT ACTIVITIES

www.adventuresofscubajack.com

TRACING

Trace the word then write it

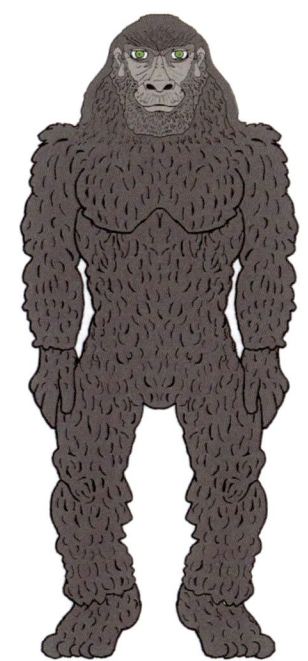

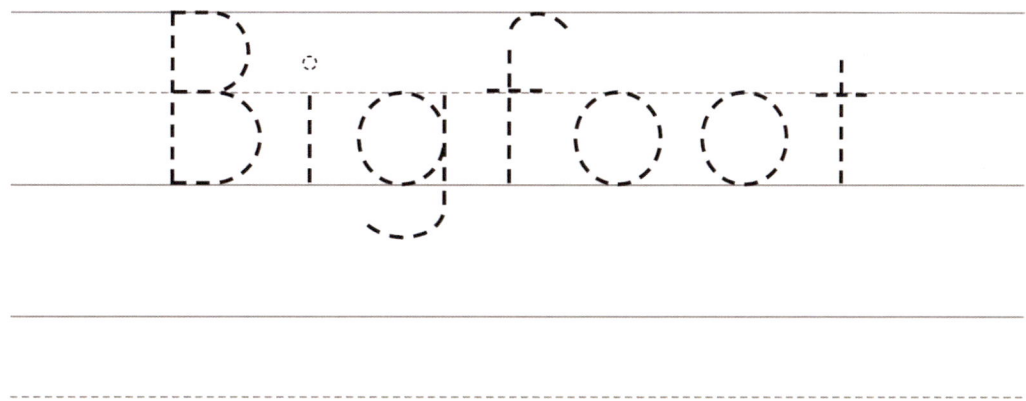

COUNTING

Count the footprints then circle the correct answer

10 12 11	14 15 16
9 10 11	12 13 14

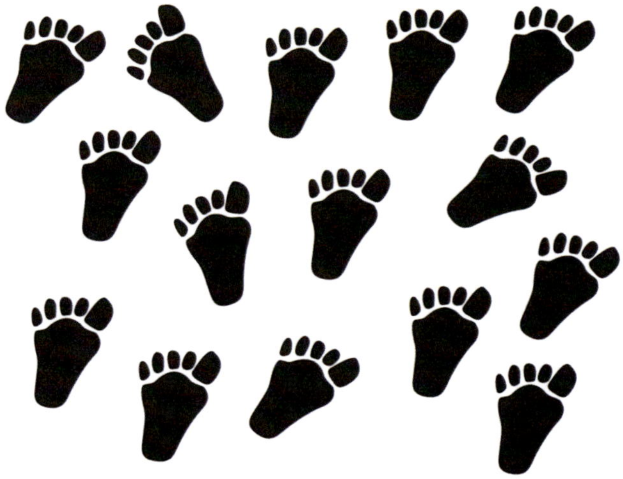

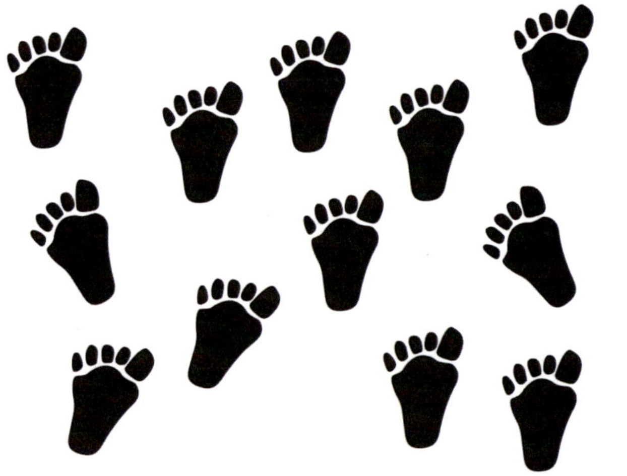

MAZE

Help the Bigfoot to find his way to the forest

BIGFOOT CRAFT

www.adventuresofscubajack.com

Let's make a Bigfoot mask together!

You will need:

Scissors
Coloring Pencils

Directions:

1- Use the scissor to cut only the discontinuous lines
2- Color your mask
3- Wear it!

VISIT US AT
WWW.ADVENTURESOFSCUBAJACK.COM

www.ingramcontent.com/pod-product-compliance
Lightning Source LLC
Chambersburg PA
CBRC090837010526
44118CB00007B/238